MW00658999

The CEO Checklist

Peter Berry

©2016 Hogan Assessment Systems, Inc.

No part of this work may be copied or transferred to any other form or expression without the expressed written consent of Hogan Assessment Systems, Inc.

www.hoganassessments.com

First printing 07-16

ISBN 978-0-692-35100-0

HOGANPRESS

Preface

Introduction to CEO Checklist

by Tomas Chamorro-Premuzic, CEO, Hogan Assessment Systems

More has been written about leadership during the past few decades than about any other aspect of human affairs. Unfortunately, however, much of this literature is based on amateurish observations and speculative insights, leaving a big gap between the science and practice of leadership. To make matters worse, the science of leadership is often inaccessible and trivial, focused on methodological minutia and obscure theories. Although leadership can be taught and developed, only a minority of leaders receive sufficient training on how to manage others and lead organisations. Indeed, most leaders must play it by ear or rely on common sense, which, as René Descartes noted more than five centuries ago, is the least common of the senses.

It is therefore very exciting to see one of the most brilliant contemporary thinkers of leadership write a compact, practical, and evidence-based guideline for modern leaders. The CEO-checklist is unique in two major ways: first, it digests the vast body of knowledge on the psychology of management and leadership; second, it translates it into concrete, business-friendly, recommendations for CEOs. If globally-minded CEOs wanted to invest only 5-min of their time to understand the key commandments of good leadership, they won't find a more useful source of knowledge than Peter Berry's definitive checklist. Having known Peter for years now, I can safely say that nobody else could have put together such a masterful and comprehensive list of data-driven recommendations for CEO, in such a concise and elegant manner.

With many decades of experience as a sought after leadership authority and proven track record as a leadership entrepreneur, Peter Berry is arguably Australia's response to Peter Drucker. He has taught, written, spoken and thought about leadership from all possible angles – as a coach, personality profiler, consultant, and mentor. His style is always direct and pragmatic; his ideas intellectually honest and effective; and his ability to bridge the gap between academic thinking and practical business solutions is rivalled by very few. I have been lucky to have Peter as a mentor and coach for some time. In a world with many theoretical experts with no practical experience, and too many practitioners who subsist only on the basis of their customers' naivety, Peter Berry is a breath of fresh air.

In short, this checklist is an indispensable resource for any CEO interested in leveraging genuine expertise on how to run an organisation more effectively. This wonderfully clever book is an antidote to all the nonsense written on the subject and an essential tool in the toolkit of any senior leader who is interested in making organisations more effective.

Ignore it only at your own peril.

Foreword
Leadership Matters
by Robert Hogan, President, Hogan Assessment Systems

The quality of people's lives depends on their careers. The quality of people's careers depends on the organisations in which their careers are embedded. The success of these organisations depends on their leadership. The effectiveness of the leadership depends on the characteristics of the people in leadership roles. Ultimately, then, personality drives leadership, leadership drives organisational performance, and who is in charge matters greatly for the fate of organisations and the people in them.

We can use this line of reasoning to improve the functioning of any organisational unit, from a football team, to a sales team, to a military team, to a city council. As obvious as this line of reasoning may seem, it is radical news to most business school professors for three reasons. First, until the mid-1990s, academics denied that personality exists, or that it affects occupational performance in any significant way. However, a series of research studies in the early 1990s showed, for those who believe in data, that people differ in meaningful ways (personality), that these differences can be assessed (personality measurement), and that these differences predict occupational performance. Second, until the early 2000s, academics denied that leadership matters. In the early 2000s, though, a series of research studies showed that personality predicts leadership performance, and leadership performance predicts team or organisational performance. The personality of the CEO is the most important determinant of firm financial performance other than the industry sector in which the firm operates. Third, as of today, academics ignore the topic of organisational effectiveness altogether. The term "organisational effectiveness" doesn't even appear in the index of any major research compendium, yet clearly Singapore has a better economy than Somalia, and South Korea has a better economy than North

Korea. Moreover, the differences in these countries' economic performance has a huge impact on the well-being of the residents there.

This argument is so important it deserves repeating. It goes as follows:

1. Personality is real: people are different, but their differences are consistent across situations, and this allows us to predict their typical behaviour.

2. Personality matters: valid measures of personality predict every consequential life outcome (e.g., health, marital satisfaction, occupational performance) better than any alternative indicator.

3. Personality predicts leadership performance better than any other alternative indicator, including IQ. But personality doesn't discriminate: Women get the same scores as men, ethnic minorities get the same scores as ethnic majorities. This means good leadership can come from anywhere.

4. Leadership predicts firm performance. Good leaders guide profitable enterprises, bad leaders ruin organisations. This is the lesson of James Collins' book "Good to Great."

The next question concerns the personality characteristics of successful leaders. The data suggests that good leaders have most or all of the following seven characteristics:

The first, and in many ways the most important characteristic, is integrity. People need to know they can trust their leaders not to betray, deceive or exploit them. This is so powerful that a team's rating of the degree to which they trust their leader is a proxy for team or business unit performance. People will not work for leaders they mistrust. Leaders need to take great care to gain and maintain the trust of their subordinates.

The second characteristic is competence — leaders need to know what they are talking about; they need to be well-grounded in the business at hand. Competence inspires trust, but more practically, staff need to be able to ask their managers for advice in solving the problems that come up constantly. In athletics, the team captain is often the best player on the team, and the best athletic managers know more about their sport than rival managers.

The third characteristic is good judgement — subordinates need to know that their leaders will take them in the right direction. In the Vietnam War, a surprising number of newly minted U.S. officers were killed by their own troops precisely because the troops thought their commanding officers would get them killed.

The fourth characteristic is vision — leaders need to be able to explain to their staff why they are doing what they are doing and why it matters. A recent DDI survey of several thousand HR managers reported that 70 percent thought the leadership of their organisation lacked any vision.

The fifth essential characteristic is ambition — wanting to be in charge and to outperform rival organisations. Ambition includes enjoying competition, wanting to win, being persistent and resilient in the face of defeat, and never being satisfied with or complacent about current levels of performance. Leaders without ambition are empty suits.

The sixth characteristic concerns "the dark side" of personality. Dark side characteristics are strengths that, when overused, turn into problems. Passion and intensity can turn into bullying and tantrums, a keen work ethic can turn into micro-management, self-confidence can turn into arrogance and inability to learn from experience. These tendencies are almost impossible to detect during interviews. Left unchecked, they will cause leaders to fail because they destroy trust.

The final characteristic is global mindedness. This characteristic is important if an organisation is operating on the world stage. It is a personality syndrome that includes being curious about other cultures and lifestyles, being tolerant of those other ways of living, and being able to adapt to strange circumstances while remaining focused on one's competitive goals.

These are the essential ingredients of leadership. Needless to say, no one person exemplifies all of these characteristics — every potential and existing leader has challenges as defined by these seven characteristics. This profile serves as a template against which people can compare their performance and determine how to improve it, provided they have the requisite ambition. People can only improve their performance if they understand their limitations.

Chapter I — The CEO Checklist

Peter Berry Consultancy (PBC) is a professional services business with more than 25 years of experience in delivering management consulting and assessment-based solutions. During this time, we have taught in business schools, presented to thousands of CEOs, and used assessments and consulting services to add value by finding solutions for clients. Peter Berry is the managing director of PBC.

Science should inform practice. To that end, we are proud to use leading-edge global assessments that are rich in research and user friendly for executives. We are the Australian distributor of the Hogan Assessments, which have heavily influenced our research and practice for more than a decade. We rely on these assessments for selection, development, self-awareness and team building.

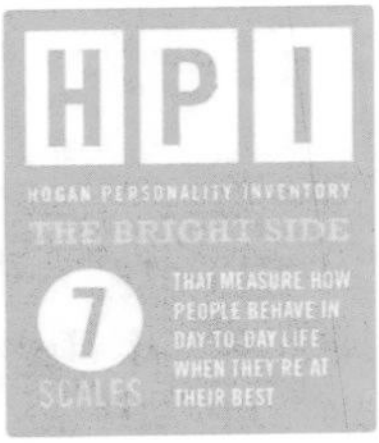

The Bright Side of Personality: Hogan Personality Inventory
A predictor for characteristic day-to-day behaviours that concern important components of all jobs. The HPI provides systematic information on personality strengths and weaknesses. This information can be used to construct a high-impact development or selection program that can have a lasting impact on a person's future success.

The Dark Side of Personality: Hogan Development Survey
An assessment that explores the characteristic ways in which a person responds to increasing pressure, stress or insecurity, and the way that person impacts others as he/she overuses coping behaviours. From this perspective, the HDS predicts behaviours that can lead to career derailment.

The Inside of Personality: Motives, Values, Preferences Inventory
Explores the core values and goals at the centre of an individual's identity. Values dictate the leader's emphasis when working with others and the type of environment the leader promotes. From this perspective, the MVPI predicts individual fit within a career, team and organisation.

In our consulting practice, we blend leadership development with business best practices and a focus on bottom-line results. We believe leadership drives engagement, and engagement drives performance. The two key chapters in this book concern building leadership performance and building business performance. We enhance performance by building capability.

What makes a great business?
What role does leadership play in growing a great business?

This book defines the key result areas in both of these categories by drawing on our research, writings and favourite business literature.

The CEO Checklist is meant to establish best practices in leadership and improve business performance. It encourages business leaders to think about next practices (moving beyond current best practices) for competitive advantage. The concept of a checklist is not new. Checklists are used in aviation and hospitals to ensure process compliance and to save lives. The CEO Checklist provides a laser focus on critical success factors for any business.

CEOs need a checklist because they can often be far too operational and not strategic. Their day-to-day experience can be one of meetings and crisis management. They often lack discipline around leadership and business excellence. They often tolerate poor-performing managers and dysfunctional teams. The checklist provides a holistic health assessment of any business.

We use business excellence frameworks to inform our consulting practice.

We have taken one of Stephen Covey's habits from the book "The 7 Habits of Highly Effective People" (Pocket Books, 2004). We have chosen the habit "sharpen the saw" because it is about self-renewal and sharpening one's tools in the search for excellence.

Our passion for continuous improvement in understanding business excellence allows for a sharp focus on the critical success factors of both leadership and business performance. Bottom line performance is driven by these two competencies. We also believe in the philosophy that less is more. As such, the information presented here is simple and succinct.

This book is called The CEO Checklist.

- The opening chapter will include The CEO Checklist and provide background.
- Chapter 2 is about building leadership performance.
- Chapter 3 relates to building business performance.

The CEO Checklist

The CEO Checklist is a road map of best practices for achieving leadership and business excellence. It can be used as an assessment tool by individual managers and management teams to:

- Assess the strengths and opportunities of the business/ business unit
- Get the difficult issues on the table for discussion
- Identify gaps in current business practices
- Identify opportunities for leadership development (assessments, programs or coaching)
- Approve an action plan that could take the business to the next level

Managers are asked to rate the 50 items as being Low, Medium or High for the business:

CEO Checklist		Low	Med	High
1.	We understand leadership drives engagement, and engagement drives performance.			
2.	Every senior manager would be reappointed tomorrow if we had to start the business again.			
3.	We have succession plans in place for all senior management positions.			
4.	Our managers have undergone personality assessments.			
5.	Our managers display strong competencies in relation to likeability and capability.			
6.	Our managers have the right balance of working in (operational) and on (strategic) the business.			
7.	Our managers have development plans to further build behavioural and business competencies.			

8.	Our managers display strong emotional intelligence through composure and appropriate social and emotional behaviours.			
9.	We use personality and cognitive testing when hiring new managers.			
10.	Our managers show high levels of resilience by demonstrating high energy and positive thoughts.			
11.	We consistently make the right judgement calls on big decisions (strategic, structural, and operational).			
12.	We understand that judgements involving people are often the most challenging; we generally get these right.			
13.	When making big decisions, we always draw from past experience.			
14.	When it comes to big decisions, we build in techniques and scenarios to manage risk and improve decision-making.			
15.	All teams are expected to be high performing, and we regularly review their culture and performance.			
16.	Our senior executive team has a great culture and is high performing.			
17.	Every year we spend money on targeted leadership programs to develop bench strength and capability.			
18.	Our business plan provides a clear vision of what winning looks like.			
19.	We have a rolling (three- to five-year) strategic plan supported by a robust one-year plan.			
20.	We have a one-page executive summary business plan, which is used to provide clarity and accountability.			
21.	Our revenue and profit performance projections look sound.			
22.	All business units/teams have second-tier plans that are aligned with the master business plan.			

23.	We have a rigorous strategic planning cycle in place.			
24.	We conduct quarterly reviews of the strategic plan.			
25.	At these reviews, we spend 50 percent of our time reviewing strategy and 50 percent building a high-performing team.			
26.	Our culture and strategy encourage innovation, and we are good at implementing new ideas.			
27.	Our results show that we are an employer of choice.			
28.	Our values are supported by behaviours; our employees know the behaviours we want and don't want.			
29.	We employ robust recruitment systems to hire the right people.			
30.	We formally induct new hires, and use a probationary period to assess both likeability and capability.			
31.	We achieve top-quartile results in our employee engagement surveys.			
32.	Our one-page plan is used as a communication tool for all employees.			
33.	The bottom 10 percent of employees are identified regularly and either improve, or are removed in a timely manner.			
34.	We give our customers a high degree of functional value around price, quality and reliability.			
35.	We give our customers a high level of emotional value around service, communications and trust.			
36.	We are a provider of choice for the majority of our customers.			
37.	Support services add significant value to our business.			
38.	The results of our customer surveys are very good.			

39.	Lifelong customer loyalty is our goal, and our high retention rate reflects that effort.			
40.	We achieve our service and operational excellence goals.			
41.	We use quality improvement tools to work toward zero defects on key processes.			
42.	We have performance standards in place for key processes so that we avoid deviations.			
43.	We work strategically with suppliers for mutual gain.			
44.	Our technology is up to date and efficient.			
45.	All teams have KPIs in place, covering areas such as financials, operations, customers and employees.			
46.	All managers are measured annually through 360° reviews, employee surveys or high-performing team assessments.			
47.	Our structure supports the strategy; we don't have any silos.			
48.	Our execution of the plan is supported by strong implementation processes.			
49.	Accountability standards are high throughout the business.			
50.	We understand that change is permanent, and we deal with people's feelings/emotions as part of the journey.			

Sometimes members of an executive team will have blind spots around the team's strengths and weaknesses. Conducting an assessment is a good way of getting hard issues on the table for debate.

The rest of this chapter will share the foundation of our CEO Checklist — research, frameworks and business literature which show business excellence and employee engagement pay off.

Business excellence and engagement deliver return on investment.

Since 1988, we have been fascinated with the world of leadership and business. In more than 25 years of consulting and teaching, we have come to the conclusion that getting leadership right is the key to getting your business right. Strategic investments in leadership often directly benefit the bottom line. However, there are also fundamental business capabilities needed for sustainability. These evolved over recent decades, and became known as best practices.

At PBC, we are impressed with the fact that business excellence and engagement deliver return on investment. The reason that organisations commit time and effort to a business excellence framework is that they are serious about continuous improvement. Studies show superior financial performance is achieved, and the work performed by global engagement survey providers proves engagement enhances sales, revenue, safety, productivity and profitability while reducing absenteeism and turnover. Engagement pays.

In 1988, the American Baldrige Business Excellence Framework was launched. For the first time, we had a balanced scorecard that gave us financial and non-financial metrics aimed at achieving superior performance.

The Baldrige Award was originally known as a quality award for which organisations could apply to measure their best practices. Typically the President of the USA would host an annual dinner and honour the winners. Some of the earlier recipients included Ritz-Carlton, Motorola and Xerox. This award was later renamed the Business Excellence Award to reflect a more holistic approach rather than focused only on quality, which was primarily related to process improvement.

The motivation behind the award was to enhance American global competitiveness, which was being challenged by overseas competition. The award quickly spawned more awards in dozens of other countries. In Australia, the Quality Award was also created in 1988, and the European Quality Awards commenced in 1992.

These frameworks pioneered the concept of strategic planning, measurement (including KPIs), customer focus, and process improvement (originally called total quality management). These concepts, which are now commonplace, were very new in the world of business. They were new practices, not best practices. The search for continuous improvement had begun. The current Baldrige framework (*Baldrige Excellence Framework: A Systems Approach to Improving Your Organization's Performance*, 2015-2016) is as follows:

1. Leadership
    - i.) Senior Leadership
    - ii.) Governance and Societal Responsibilities
2. Strategy
    - i.) Strategy Development
    - ii.) Strategy Implementation
3. Customers
    - i.) Voice of the Customer
    - ii.) Customer Engagement
4. Measurement, Analysis and Knowledge Management
    - i.) Measurement, Analysis and Improvement of
    - ii.) Organisational Performance
    - iii.) Knowledge Management, Information, and Information
    - iv.) Technology

5. Workforce
   i.) Workforce Environment
   ii.) Workforce Engagement
6. Operations
   i.) Work Processes
   ii.) Operational Effectiveness
7. Results
   i.) Product and Process Results
   ii.) Customer-Focused Results
   iii.)Workforce-Focused Results
   iv.) Leadership and Governance Results
   v.) Financial and Market Results

CHECKPOINT 1

We understand leadership drives engagement, and engagement drives performance.

We should note in the "Workforce" and "Customers" categories, we are specifically looking for engagement. Category 7 looks for a balanced scorecard set of results.

You will note that leadership is the number one category in the model. We happen to agree that leadership is the engine room for business excellence. Leadership can be measured and improved.

In 1996, Kaplan and Norton wrote "The Balanced Scorecard" (Harvard Business Review). The groundbreaking concept here was to establish non-financial measures alongside financial ones as a basis for strategic planning, measurement and continuous improvement. Up until this time, the only measures most organisations used were financial (e.g., budgets and profit and loss). The balanced scorecard has four components:

1. Financial
2. Customer
3. Internal Processes
4. Learning and Growth

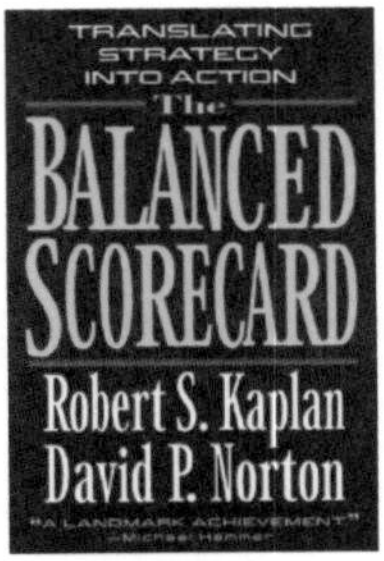

While the Kaplan/Norton model is deservedly world famous for adding non-financial metrics to the financials, there is one huge limitation: Leadership, people and culture are missing. We find their balanced scorecard too narrowly defined, as it misses the fundamental point about leadership driving engagement and engagement driving results. We have heard some argue people can be captured under the "Learning and Growth" category, but we doubt this was the original intention. We are still left with the challenge of how to improve and measure leadership and culture. When we work with clients around balanced scorecards, we simply add actions and measures specifically about leadership, culture and people to compensate.

Just to make the point one more time, because leadership is not overtly in the Kaplan/Norton model, they have dumbed down the whole field of leadership and its impact. The challenge right now is how to measure leadership effectiveness and how to review and reward it. Far too many organisations are still rewarding performance (sales and operational KPIs) and ignoring the behavioural component around living the values and delivering engagement. The performance of a team should be a more important metric than the individual performance of the manager. Leaders should be measured by and remunerated for the performance and culture of their team.

The Baldrige framework and the balanced scorecard have been the premier business models over the past three decades. We prefer the Baldrige model because of its emphasis on leadership, people and culture, which is not obvious in the balanced scorecard.

In the 1990s, the Baldrige organisation conducted a study to examine how award winners perform with respect to accounting, profitability and market metrics. The study used industry benchmarks and a control group of similar firms. The study found the following:

> "Our results suggest that award winners perform significantly better when compared with a group of similar-sized firms and the industry benchmarks in terms of

> accounting and financial performance measures. Award winners are valued 11 percent higher than otherwise-comparable firms in the control sample. This suggests the award winners are superior financial performers and are valued higher by investors."

Over the years it has become very apparent to us that best practice is best captured when we see behavioural competencies around engagement and business competencies around performance. These two concepts provide the opportunity to assess individual leaders, to evaluate teams, and to measure organisations.

In the late 1990s, organisations started using employee opinion surveys to measure the level of satisfaction and engagement in the workplace. Many organisations take employee engagement seriously and aim to be an employer of choice or a great place to work. A number of organisations have developed employee value propositions to attract, on-board and retain the right people.

Our research shows a direct correlation between employee engagement and business performance. For a global retailer, we found high engagement mapped to superior sales and productivity, and also to staff retention and low absenteeism. Indeed, in highly engaged stores staff turnover was only 10 percent, while in disengaged stores turnover was 70 percent. Our research showed the store manager and assistant store manager had the biggest impact on the level of engagement.

In the survey, one of the questions we ask is "Would you leave the organisation if offered another job or would you not leave the organisation if offered another job?" Of the respondents, 36 percent said they would leave, and 64 percent said they would stay. The engagement levels were 62 percent for the employees who would go, and 74 percent for those who would stay (the all-industries average is 71 percent). This demonstrates a clear correlation between engagement and retention.

CHECK- POINT 2

Every senior manager would be reappointed tomorrow if we had to start the business again.

Our survey results show one in three people would leave to take a job with another organisation. They typically score 10 or more percentage points lower than the engaged group, and they often choose to stay in a job for the convenience factor — the money is okay, the hours are fine, and it is close to home. The danger is the cost associated with significant turnover. Another danger is that seriously negative people are spreading their misery to good people.

Three overarching factors emerged when the data from people who would leave was examined. First, employees want to quit because of their manager. They say the manager lacks people skills, does not make them feel valued, and may be temperamental, or a bully. Second, they want to quit because of the workplace culture. They say there is favouritism, double standards, poor performance and poor communication. Third, they want to quit because of the job. They say the job is not the right one for them, and their job satisfaction is not enough to retain them.

Staff turnover is thereby caused by leadership. It is a leadership responsibility to hold managers accountable for their behaviour. It is a leadership responsibility to create a strong culture of engagement in teams. It is a leadership responsibility to ensure selection systems hire the right people.

Aon Hewitt and Gallup are two of the largest global engagement businesses. Their substantial research supports the proposition that engagement pays, and leaders make a significant contribution to engagement. Aon Hewitt defines engagement as "the psychological state and behavioural outcomes that lead to better performance." They measure three elements of employee engagement:

1. Say; speak positively about the organisation
2. Stay; want to be part of the organisation
3. Strive; desire to go above and beyond in their job

With seven million employees over a five-year rolling database, Aon Hewitt found that 67 percent of employees speak positively about their organisation, 56 percent want to stay with their organisation, and 58 percent strive to go above and beyond in their role. The "stay" statistic of 56 percent is similar to the PBC finding that 64 percent would not take a job with another organisation.

CHECKPOINT 3

We have succession plans in place for all senior management positions.

Aon Hewitt's research also shows 61 percent of employees are engaged. Of the 39 percent who are not engaged, 23 percent are ambivalent about their employer, and 16 percent are actively disengaged — these employees "actively destroy value through negativity across the Say, Stay and Strive elements."

Aon Hewitt claims that leaders hold the key to employee engagement. They state that:

> *Engaging leaders think, feel and act in different ways than do typical leaders. Leaders have a multiplier effect on engagement in that they affect engagement through control over all the top drivers, in addition to having a direct effect on the engagement of others through their interactions.*

Their research shows that engagement has a positive impact on business outcomes. These include:

1. Positive financial indicators including revenue, sales growth and shareholder return.
2. Customer engagement expressed through higher retention and better net promoter scores.
3. Operational indicators including productivity and safety.
4. Employee indicators including retention, absenteeism and wellness.

The Gallup organisation tells a similar story. Their data shows the following statistics about an engaged workplace:

1. 37% lower absenteeism
2. 25% lower turnover (in high-turnover organisations)
3. 65% lower turnover (in low-turnover organisations)
4. 48% fewer safety incidents
5. 10% higher customer metrics
6. 21% higher productivity
7. 22% higher profitability

Our philosophy is leadership drives engagement, and engagement drives results. Sirota is a global provider of employee engagement surveys. They have clients including Dell, Shell and Hilton Hotels and they survey between 1 and 1.5 million employees annually. Their research shows employee engagement impacts business performance. Engagement drives efficiency, innovation, customer service and sales performance. They claim management has the biggest impact on engagement, followed by team culture and individual fit. This supports our own findings from employee surveys.

Sirota's best practice around engagement is:

- Senior leaders recognise the value of employee engagement.
- Senior leaders have engagement as a KPI.
- The business is effective at measuring engagement.
- Leaders know how to act on the engagement data.
- Leaders understand the role they play in improving engagement and performance.

In July-August 2008, the *Harvard Business Review* published an article called "Putting the Service-Profit Chain to Work." The research shows the relationships between profitability, customer loyalty, and employee satisfaction, loyalty and productivity. The authors claim that employee engagement creates value and satisfaction for customers. Loyal customers then contribute to revenue growth and profitability. This fits with our philosophy that engaged employees create engaged customers, which delivers positive outcomes around bottom-line results, including absenteeism, turnover, sales and productivity.

In recent years, we conducted significant research around the issue of effective leadership. One piece of research involved looking at 1,600 managers who took part in 360° reviews. We picked the top 30 and the bottom 30 managers. Both groups had "hardworking" and "knowledge" in their strengths, suggesting that they have the competence to deliver against their job description. The high-scoring managers also had "good people skills" and "enthusiastic/positive attitude." These two items did not appear as strengths for the managers with low scores. The high scorers were also described as "positive role models" and demonstrated "good leadership skills." These two were also absent in the low-scoring managers' results.

In the "Opportunities to Improve" section of the 360° review, the high-scoring managers had "takes on too much/spread self too thin," "delegate more," and "challenge poor performers" as the key issues. The low-scoring managers were told they need to "improve people skills/interpersonal skills," "communicate better," and improve their "time management and organisational skills."

The one big takeaway here is the significance of people skills. For the lower-scoring managers, it is clear that they struggle with relationship skills. To a lesser degree, they also struggle with resilience by sometimes being aggressive or negative. In short, they lack emotional competencies around people skills and resilience. They lack self-awareness, self-regulation and the motivation to improve.

A second study involved 680 managers and drew upon Hogan 360° data and Hogan EQ results. One of the Hogan EQ scales is called "Influence." It measures the degree to which a person seems able to intentionally affect others' moods, thoughts and behaviours. When we analysed the managers' assessment of the manager being rated, high influencing skills were seen to be related to communication and people skills. Dr Robert Hogan describes leadership as "the ability to get along to get ahead." We sometimes define leadership as "getting better results through better relationships." Influencing skills are a critical component of making one more socially effective at work. Influencing others is about engaging minds and hearts. Influence is getting others to say "yes."

When we looked at what all of the raters (managers, peers and direct reports) said about the 680 leaders, the two 360° categories that had the strongest correlation with a high EQ score were "Resilience" and "People Skills." Resilience is defined as being calm, steady, approachable and not temperamental, aggressive or moody. People skills are defined as making others feel valued by being warm and thoughtful in relationships, rather than engaging in rude or bullying behaviours. These two scales form the basis of self-management and relationship management.

The third study considered Hogan personality assessments and Hogan 360° results for 476 managers. PBC identified the key requirements of managers, peers and reports in terms of 360° competencies. Managers of the managers said that the most important competencies were communication, people skills and resilience. The peers were looking for resilience and people skills. Direct reports reported resilience, people skills and integrity as most important. All three rater groups focused on resilience and people skills. We also found that direct reports do not like managers who are temperamental, moody or explosive.

The evidence is clear. A commitment to business excellence and engagement builds healthier cultures, happier clients and a stronger bottom line.

Chapter 2 — Building Leadership Performance

In this chapter, we will focus on the six key result areas of building effective leadership.

1. Measuring, Understanding and Improving Your Brand
Brand is one's reputation as seen by observers. It is critical to one's success. Brand involves both behavioural and business competencies. It starts with self-awareness, which is best achieved through personality assessments, 360° feedback, coaching and practice. One needs to be motivated and disciplined to improve competence, confidence and reputation. A person's brand is ultimately what they choose it to be.
2. Getting Rid of Bad Habits and Adding New Habits
Good **habits** are competencies that make an individual more effective. It is about being likeable and capable. Competencies can be developed from self-awareness. One needs feedback to discover what to keep doing, stop doing and start doing. Habits can be personal (exercise) and professional (setting goals/KPIs). They can be learned and become second nature. But remember, the brain is a slow learner, it takes a lot of practice and persistence.
3. Building Emotional Intelligence (EQ) Competencies
Everyone has a natural level of **EQ.** More importantly, emotional competencies can be learned if one is motivated to do better. These competencies relate to people and social skills, and managing emotions maturely (i.e. getting along to get ahead). The goal is to demonstrate intra- and inter-personal skills so that one is engaged and engaging. Being resilient and warm gets people connected, builds trust and enables one to influence others.

4. Being Resilient
Using **positive energy and thoughts** to cope with turbulence and disruption is critical to sustainable performance. We want people to be in the high-performance zone by practicing recovery ("Me Time" for rest and renewal). The goal is to avoid stress and burnout, which impacts 70 percent of managers in their careers. Energy is expended and must be recovered. Human beings are not machines.
5. Exercising Good Judgement
Consistently **making the right call** when it comes to big decisions is crucial. Managers must focus on getting key business decisions right, especially concerning strategy, staffing and operations. Risk management is crucial. People judgements can be some of the hardest. Good judgement is not an inherent trait for most people, but rather a skill that can be developed. Half of all decisions end in failure, and can damage one's brand.
6. Building a High-Performing Team
Leading and sustaining a **high-performing team** is the ultimate measure of a leader. Business is about delivering results. Teams deliver results. Therefore, a leader should be measured by the culture and performance of their team. Many teams are dysfunctional, which impacts business performance. The concept of "one team, one plan" is critical to getting everyone on the same page. Assessing team strengths and weaknesses is the key to improvement.

Measuring, Understanding and Improving Your Brand

Leaders, teams, organisations and products have a brand. Brand is reputation and it is the most important asset that one can have. Brand is measurable (360˚) and explainable (personality assessments). Improving your brand is always possible. It starts with assessments, self-awareness and the motivation and persistence to improve competencies. In time, confidence and reputation will grow as the competencies kick in. For example, emotional intelligence can be improved through learned social and emotional behaviours that are necessary to be successful in the workplace. Judgement and decision-making can also be improved through better risk management techniques.

CHECKPOINT 4

Our managers have undergone personality assessments.

In their book "The Human Brand" (Jossey-Bass, 2013), Malone and Fiske state that how people relate to other people, products and companies is based on their brand. The book makes the following key points:

1. Every brand is human, and every human is a brand.

2. Warmth and competence are key to your brand.

3. Warmth creates engagement so that competence can drive performance.

The authors claim "to exert influence, you must balance competence with warmth." The authors say the chance that a manager who is strongly disliked will be considered a good leader is only 1 in 2,000.

Our key takeaway from this book is brands are built on warmth and competence. This maps to our leadership model around behavioural and business competencies.

We are indebted to our friend Dr Tomas Chamorro-Premuzic, the CEO of Hogan Assessments, for introducing us to the confidence-competence cycle, modified as follows:

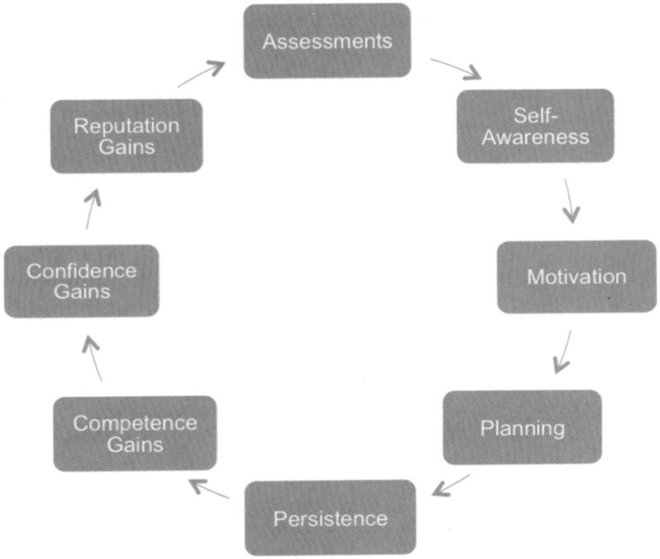

Typically, the journey to understand and improve one's brand starts with assessments. The best assessments consist of a personality profile and 360° review. We then test for the level of self-awareness and try to identify one's motivation to change and do better. Without reaching serious agreement around the motivation, some people pay lip service to a program or coaching. We have six basic questions when maximising the coaching opportunity for success:

1. What do you want your brand to be?
2. What do you need to keep/stop/start doing?
3. What is your motivation to change and improve?
4. Are you serious about the effort and the journey?
5. What help do you need?
6. Who can give you this help?

Our coaching interventions focus on two to three goals for each individual. Any more than this, and the process becomes complicated and difficult.

Next comes the persistence and resilience to keep doing your daytime job as well as your personal improvement. The competence gains come from internalising the changes, understanding that practice makes perfect and making the changes stick. The confidence gains come from the new competencies becoming second nature, people trusting your capabilities and you becoming a more engaging co-worker. The reputation gains come from having a stronger brand, better relationships and more effective displays of efficiency. The end result is more likeability and capability.

CHECKPOINT 7

Our managers have development plans to further build behavioural and business competencies.

In "The Speed of Trust" by Stephen Covey (Simon & Schuster, 2006), high-performing managers build trust through character and competence. Covey says this enables them to get things done faster. He defines character as integrity, motivation and the right attitudes towards people. Competence includes skills, capabilities, work habits and work products. This helped PBC confirm that we were on the right track in measuring both behavioural and business competencies.

In the book "What Got You Here Won't Get You There" (Hyperion, 2007), Goldsmith made the obvious point that technical and cognitive capability will get you going up the ladder, but behavioural competencies will take you further. His book made the following important points:

1. The higher your level of success, the more destructive your bad habits become.
2. Stopping a bad behaviour can be more productive than doing something right.
3. The higher up you go in the organisation, the more you need to make other people winners and not make it about winning yourself.
4. We can't see in ourselves what we can see so clearly in others.
5. As human beings, we almost always suffer from a disconnect between the self we think we are and the self the rest of the world sees in us.
6. The best method for identifying strengths and weaknesses is 360° feedback.

Jack Welch became very famous in the 1990s as the CEO of General Electric. At that time, they were the biggest company in the world. Whether we like Jack Welch or not, he made a very powerful and simple point about evaluating managers. We can assess them using two criteria: Do they live the values, and do they deliver the numbers? This is keeping it really simple and it's absolutely right. Welch also took leadership very seriously. In his book, "Winning" (HarperCollins, 2005), he states, "Before you are a leader, success is all about growing yourself. When you become a leader, success is all about growing others."

When we teach at business schools or coach people, we like to be succinct and use easy to understand frameworks. When all is said and done, one's success in life will be driven by likeability and capability. These two competencies are the bottom line to one's ability to set goals and achieve them through others. These people can build trust and engagement.

Getting Rid of Bad Habits and Adding New Habits

Thirty years ago, Stephen Covey wrote the classic book, "The 7 Habits of Highly Effective People" (Pocket Books, 2004). The key word here is habits. In other words, behavioural and business competencies can be developed. It may take years of practice, but eventually one's competence and confidence grow. So does one's reputation. It is no different from children learning to ride a bike, drive a car or study hard.

We often come across people who say they are part of a Toastmasters group to develop their confidence around public speaking. They tell us public speaking will never come naturally, but they have developed some basic competencies that allow them to get by.

The good news about personality and emotional intelligence is that they do not define our careers or restrict our capabilities. Learned social and emotional competencies are critical. Self-awareness and self-management are the starting points to engage constructively in relationships. Resilience (i.e., emotional stability, good energy levels, and positive thoughts) is very important.

We then look for relationship management skills, which Goleman described as empathy and social skills. We look for the ability of people to read others like a book, the ability to understand the emotional makeup of others, and social skills for building and maintaining relationships. Our research shows that communication and people skills are the key to influencing others.

Covey says, "You are what you habitually do, so adopt productive habits." He also says that "excellence is a habit, not an aptitude." With this thinking in mind, he challenges readers to work on their ability to improve habits and their lives.

In "The Power of Habit" by Charles Duhigg (Random House, 2012), the author claims that:

- Life is a mass of habits — 40 percent of actions each day are from habits.
- The brain converts a sequence of actions into routine.
- The real power of habit is the insight that your habits are what you choose them to be.

Life is, indeed, often a series of habits. For example, many of us have a set routine in the morning. This enables the brain to cruise and save its energy for issues when attention is really required. The limbic system is a slow learner. It takes a lot of practice and persistence to develop new competencies. It takes a lot of perseverance for new habits to become second nature. It also takes a lot of effort to control or eliminate bad habits.

We challenge our clients to identify bad habits that need to be removed, and new habits that will increase their effectiveness at work. We work with many management teams on how to create more robust strategic planning cycles, set goals/KPIs, challenge poor performers and be more resilient. In time and with practice, competencies are developed which become an acquired behaviour. The key to a development plan is having good quality assessments so one knows where to improve. This often involves personality assessments and 360° reviews.

Practice makes perfect. Daniel Goleman talks about the "10,000 hour rule" where if you truly want to be world class at something, you need to invest 10,000 hours of practice. This could apply to golf or playing a musical instrument. Luckily, we don't need 10,000 hours to build basic workplace competencies. The keys to improvement are being motivated to succeed, having a development plan, and the support to make it a reality.

In Covey's book, "The Speed of Trust" (Free Press, 2006), he talks about every relationship having a trust account. He says that how you behave can add to or subtract from how much people trust you. His 13 behaviours need to become habits:

1. **Talk straight** — Say what you mean; mean what you say.
2. **Demonstrate respect** — Do small things that acknowledge and express respect and appreciation.
3. **Create transparency** — Create transparency by being truthful and disclosing your intentions openly and verifiably.
4. **Right wrongs** — Fix what you have broken, forgive others, and be humble.
5. **Show loyalty** — Give others credit for what they have done, both to their faces and behind their backs.
6. **Deliver results** — When you commit, deliver results — not excuses.
7. **Get better** — Make a commitment to improve yourself, then act consistently to fulfil that commitment.
8. **Confront reality** — Have the courage to face hard facts and bring out the truths that others may be afraid to voice.
9. **Clarify expectations** — Make everyone's expectations crystal clear.
10. **Practice accountability** — Pay attention to what you think and say, and stop any tendency to blame others.
11. **Listen first** — Listening demonstrates respect and provides the knowledge you need to make the best possible decisions.
12. **Keep commitments** — The more commitments you make and keep, the more trust you build.
13. **Extend trust** — Build trust in a relationship by trusting the others involved.

Building Emotional Intelligence (EQ) Competencies

One of the most important points made by Daniel Goleman is that emotional competencies can be developed, no matter what the level of emotional intelligence might be. Emotional competencies involve both emotional and social competencies.

Emotional intelligence can be defined as being able to perceive, identify and manage emotions effectively in yourself and others. It is about using your emotions intelligently to get the best out of yourself. In the early phases of one's career, it is probably cognitive ability, technical skills and work ethic that accelerates one's progress. But eventually, if you are leading people and client facing, social and emotional competencies will enable you to stand out from the crowd.

In the 1930s, the first research on emotional intelligence began around total intelligence beyond one's intellect. In 1983, Howard Gardner began writing about multiple intelligence. He wrote that intrapersonal and interpersonal intelligence are as important as the type of intelligence typically measured by IQ and related tests. The research suggested that leaders who are able to establish mutual trust, respect and a certain warmth and rapport will be more effective.

CHECKPOINT 8

Our managers display strong emotional intelligence through composure and appropriate social and emotional behaviours.

Salovey and Mayer coined the term "emotional intelligence" in 1990. They described emotional intelligence as a form of social intelligence around one's own and others' feelings and emotions, and the ability to use this to guide one's thinking and action.

In 1995, Daniel Goleman popularised the concept with his book "Emotional Intelligence: Why It Can Matter More Than IQ" (Bantam Books).

Goleman claimed that 80 percent of one's success in a career can be associated with emotional intelligence.

One of the points we like about Goleman's work is his distinction between emotional intelligence and emotional competence. He describes emotional intelligence as a natural level of intelligence that varies from one person to the next. He defines emotional competence as being a learned capability relating to personal and social skills that lead to superior performance at work. He defines five key areas of emotional competence:

1. **Self-Awareness**
    - The ability to recognise and understand your moods, emotions and drives, as well as their effect on others.
2. **Self-Regulation**
    - The ability to control or redirect disruptive impulses and moods.
    - The propensity to suspend judgement — to think before acting.
3. **Motivation**
    - A passion to work for reasons that go beyond money or status.
    - A propensity to pursue goals with energy and persistence.
4. **Empathy**
    - The ability to understand the emotional makeup of other people.
    - Skill in treating people according to their emotional reactions.
5. **Social Skills**
    - Proficiency in managing relationships and building networks.
    - An ability to find common ground and build rapport.

We often use this model by asking participants to identify which of these items would improve their EQ.

Every day, people are confronted with hundreds of stimuli that trigger emotional responses. The brain has the capacity to learn how to filter and interpret these emotions so that socially appropriate behaviour is the outcome. We coach our clients to understand the importance of using a filter in the brain. The filter regulates emotions and produces rational behaviour. People who do not use a filter lack self-awareness and self-regulation. The following image helps explain how emotional stimulations need to be filtered to produce socially appropriate behaviour.

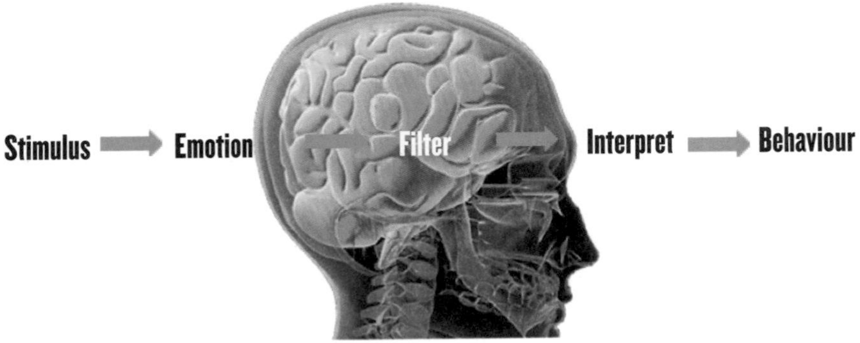

Understanding and using the filter has helped many of our clients to improve their EQ. When emotional or stressed, the self-talk is around using the filter. The ability to manage feelings and handle stress is also key to presenting with emotional intelligence. Goleman talks about mastering specific skills that allow for greater effectiveness at work. Based on our previous research, these are largely behavioural competencies built on resilience and people skills.

CHECKPOINT 9

We use personality and cognitive testing when hiring new managers.

Our Hogan 360° research shows that high-scoring managers have the following four competencies as part of their brand:

1. Strong work ethic, hardworking
2. Experienced, knowledgeable and capable
3. A positive and enthusiastic attitude
4. Good people skills, strong interpersonal skills

Items one and two relate to capability.
Items three and four constitute likeability.

The Hogan philosophy is that individuals with higher EQ:

- Quickly understand what others feel and why they behave in a certain way.
- Are rewarding to deal with, rarely moody or argumentative.
- Remain calm in stressful situations and handle pressure well.
- Tend to be enthusiastic about work and remain optimistic.

CHECKPOINT 10

Our managers show high levels of resilience by consistently demonstrating high energy and positive thoughts.

CHECKPOINT 11

We consistently make the right judgement calls on big decisions (strategic, structural, and operational).

EQ matters because it is responsible for a significant component of one's performance:

- Traditional tools measuring cognitive intelligence don't tell us everything about one's success in life.
- Global competency research shows one-third of the difference in performance of people is due to technical skills and cognitive ability, while two-thirds is due to emotional competence.
- In top leadership positions, four-fifths of the difference is due to EQ.

The goal is to demonstrate intrapersonal and interpersonal skills so one is both engaged and engaging.

Being Resilient

We use a resilience model written by Marty and Joshua Seldman called "Executive Stamina: How to Optimize Time, Energy, and Productivity to Achieve Peak Performance" (John Wiley & Sons, 2008). It focuses on five key elements of one's personal and professional life:

- Work/Life Alignment — aligning time to what is truly important.
- Health and Wellness — integrating healthy practices into daily life.
- Job Productivity — staying in control with high-payoff activities.
- Career Management — taking control of your career.
- Maintenance of Positive Relationships — making time for them.

The resilience model is aimed at people taking control of their lives, having goals and building the energy and focus to stay on top.

Turbulence and disruption are the new business paradigms, and never before have individuals, teams and organisations experienced so many shocks and challenges. In the next decade, successful companies will be those who survive and prosper by reinventing themselves. If change is the new business paradigm, then resilience has to be a very important leadership capability. It should be part of any leadership competency model and any leadership development program.

The Seldmans uniquely capture the key for managers to avoid stress and burnout by embracing the "sprint — marathon — recovery cycle" to stay in what they call the high-performance zone. They define the sprint as the year ahead, the marathon as one's career, and the recovery cycle as one's rest, recreation, nutrition and fitness disciplines. Taking dedicated time out to recover will get you back into the performance zone quicker than others. Too many people feel guilty about having me time, yet it is critical for being at your best in relationships at work and home.

Never before have people given so much energy to their job and relationships. Energy is expended and must be renewed. The key to recovery is renewal of energy to avoid burnout. Everyone needs to have a stress management program to get the best out of life. Human beings are not machines.

One part of the Seldman model is the performance zone/ recovery nexus:

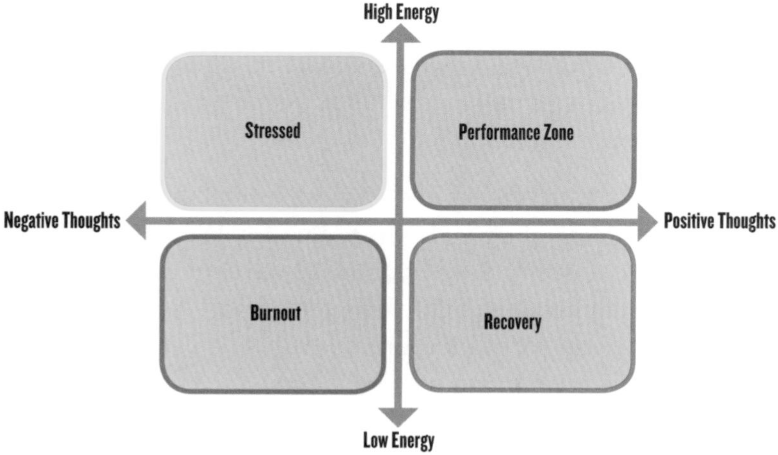

The goal is to consistently stay in the high-performance zone where high energy and positive thoughts allow us the most effectiveness at work and home. We stay here longer by practicing recovery, which is defined as rest and renewal. This is what elite sporting teams do in between games. It has been scientifically proven. Otherwise, one can easily become stressed and burned out.

Recovery programs vary enormously. Many of our clients talk about exercise, nutrition, sleep, hobbies, meditation and family time as a means of recovery. Some talk specifically about golf, swimming, running, surfing and yoga. Others talk about time on a motorbike, playing with children, gardening, watching television and listening to music.

Dedicated recovery programs should be a natural, disciplined part of one's life. Taking time to recover should not create feelings of guilt, because recovery makes for more effective relationships. If a person's operating rhythm around high performance and recovery is not right, they will end up on the left-hand side of the model. Up to 70 percent of people tell me they were there at different stages of their career. Sometimes the victim mentality kicks in, where everyone else is to blame.

Our research shows more effective workload management, challenging poor performers, and better use of meeting times are three of the biggest challenges. Better workload management involves setting priorities, having a checklist, delegation and stronger time management. It requires a sharp focus on what is really important.

Challenging poor performers is rarely done well, but is a great source of frustration to team members. We encourage organisations to identify their bottom 10 percent and to improve or remove these people in a 90-day cycle. Good companies identify the poor performers every quarter and set about building capability to deal with these people.

Meetings can also be a major problem. Too many meetings lack agendas, don't deliver outcomes, lack good time management, have more participants than necessary, and can be poorly chaired. Meetings must have a purpose. We need to separate tactical meetings from strategic meetings, and this is best done by establishing an annual meeting operating rhythm which defines which meetings are tactical and which ones are strategic. Many PBC clients are reviewing their meetings to improve efficiency.

CHECKPOINT 12

We understand that judgements involving people are often the most challenging; we generally get these right.

Exercising Good Judgement

CHECKPOINT 13

When making big decisions, we always draw from past experience.

Good decision-making is a critical component of effective leadership. When it comes to big decisions, judgement calls can make or break an individual, a team or an organisation. Everyone has a natural personality preference when making decisions. Self-awareness is critical to understanding what needs to be added or subtracted to one's decision-making style, especially when making a big call. As many as 50 percent of decisions end in failure. Think about how many:

- Staffing decisions end up being wrong.
- Strategic decisions do not work.
- Poor subcontractors have been hired.
- Marketing campaigns under-deliver.
- Critical processes go wrong.

Key business decisions live in four boxes: strategic, staffing, operational and organisational.

In "Judgment: How Winning Leaders Make Great Calls" (Portfolio, 2009), Tichy and Bennis claim that the fundamental essence of leadership is the ability to make good judgement calls consistently, especially when the stakes are high, information is limited, and the right call is far from obvious. Good judgement is not an inborn trait, but rather a skill that can be developed, refined and nurtured throughout an organisation. Leaders will be remembered for their best and worst judgement calls. They say judgements involving people can be some of the hardest. They quote Wayne Downing, a retired four-star general who ran the United States Army Special Forces, who said, "Most of my bad judgement calls were generally about people."

Ohio State University Professor Paul Nutt spent 20 years studying how decisions are made. In his book, "Why Decisions Fail" (Berret-Koehler Publishers, 2002), his key finding is that decisions fail half of the time. People making decisions often lack sufficient knowledge and use faulty decision-making styles. They can also fail to execute effectively.

Personality plays a big part in decision-making. Over-confidence and under-confidence can bring different negatives to the decision-making table. Being in denial can also be the enemy of good decision-making. Sometimes there is value in examining previous bad decisions to avoid making mistakes in the future. Even better, we should learn from the mistakes of others.

David Goldsmith articulates a five-step process that captures critical thinking in "Problem Solved! The Secrets of Decision Making and Problem Solving" (Create Space Independent Publishing Platform, 2014):

1. Observations — looking at a problem from every possible angle.
2. Experience — benefiting from everything you have already tried and learned.
3. Evaluation — staying open-minded and thinking strategically.
4. Analysis — the process of assessing your assumptions and judgement calls.
5. Explanation — how you arrive at a logical understanding of your situation.

This five-step process can enhance the risk management necessary on big calls.

Some of the literature talks about "system one" and "system two" thinking. The mind uses two cognitive systems. System one is intuitive and emotional, works easily and automatically, and does not take much effort. It makes quick judgements based on familiar patterns and one's experience. System two thinking is rational and methodical. It takes more effort, requires intense focus, and operates methodically. It defines the problem, decides what is important, generates alternatives, and signs off on the best solution. These two systems interact continually, but not always smoothly. The challenge is to know when to use each of the systems in our decision-making.

CHECKPOINT 14

When it comes to big decisions, we build in techniques and scenarios to manage risk and improve decision-making.

We also like the concept of the 90/10 rule, where 90 percent of the decision-making energy should go to the top 10 percent of decisions that are critical. This applies to business and home. If we get the big decisions right, it doesn't matter so much if we get one or two of the smaller issues wrong. We encourage teams to reflect on decisions they have gotten right and wrong in the past, and then ask them to identify the critical decisions that they must get right in the next 12 months. We like to use the following questions in a management workshop:

1. What are the big calls we got right in the last five years?
2. What are the big calls we got wrong in the last five years?
3. What are the big decisions we must get right in the next year?

This creates some very interesting conversations, which is very real to the people in the business. It confirms that judgement is a critical leadership competency. We also like to challenge individual managers to think about judgement in their personal lives. This could mean reflecting on the decisions they got right or wrong, but more importantly, the big decisions they need to get right in the next year (family, financial, medical, etc.).

There are four business domains requiring serious judgement — strategy, people, operations and organisation. In the strategy box, we ask them to have a long-term view (three to five years) and a one-year plan around what winning looks like. For the private sector, it is typically top-line and bottom-line financials (revenue and profit), and the new products and markets that will generate extra business. For the public sector, it is how they make a difference and how they can be the industry leader. Strategy can also involve considerations of mergers and acquisitions. Many of these have gone wrong. Strategy must also include non-financial aspects, such as people and customer engagement, and service/operational excellence.

CHECKPOINT 15

All teams are expected to be high performing, and we regularly review their culture and performance.

Staffing issues are critical and often the most difficult. Staffing best practices include recruiting, inducting, motivating and retaining high-performing individuals. We sometimes call this the "hire hard, manage easy" approach. Improving or removing poor performers is also critical. This repeatedly comes up in 360° reviews and engagement surveys. Succession planning is also a major challenge. Finding the right CEO can be tortuous. Aiming to be an employer of choice and to create a great place to work should be a no-brainer. Only 10 percent of organisations have superior levels of engagement. Staff disengagement and turnover is driven by poor managers, poor team culture and wrong job fit.

The big operational decisions involve efficient processes and systems to deliver customer expectations by getting it right the first time, every time. The goal is to achieve service/operational excellence where rework is the enemy. Lean process management strategies can help with cost, cycle time and waste reduction. Six Sigma projects can boost defect reduction, eliminate variation and improve processes. Effective supply-chain management involves working strategically with suppliers and partners. Despite their best efforts, many organisations make the wrong decisions around processes, process

JUDGEMENT

Decision-Making

How you learn, how you decide, and how you adapt

Do you make good decisions?

improvement, procurement and subcontractors. The challenge is to continuously improve key processes to achieve performance levels and avoid deviations. Safety can be a big issue for some.

The big organisational issues are typically around strategy, structure, culture and leadership. It starts with having a high-performing team at the top of the pyramid, as well as throughout the organisation. Decisions around the structure are paramount. Many organisations have silos where the left hand does not collaborate with the right hand. How many times does sales fight with marketing or maintenance arm wrestle with production?

CHECKPOINT 16

Our senior executive team has a great culture and is high performing.

The right organisational values and behaviours are needed to drive the culture, and managers must be role models. Innovation and technology decisions can also be big-ticket items.

The Hogan Judgement Report captures one's thinking and decision-making style. It evaluates how we process information, how we make decisions, and how we typically react to feedback about decisions. This report is invaluable in creating self-awareness and team building.

Building a High-Performing Team

Dr Robert Hogan proposes the purpose of leadership is to drive results, and teams actually produce the results, therefore, a manager should be measured by the performance of their team. Teams can easily be dysfunctional. A bad leader or a difficult team member can kill engagement and performance.

In the next five years, the need for high-performing teams will appear as goals in strategic business plans. Teams can be assessed and improved. It can also be a KPI.

Patrick Lencioni, in "The Five Dysfunctions of a Team" (Wiley, 2002), states high-performing teams have the following traits:

- Trust
- Unfiltered conflict
- Timely decision-making
- Accountability
- Collective results

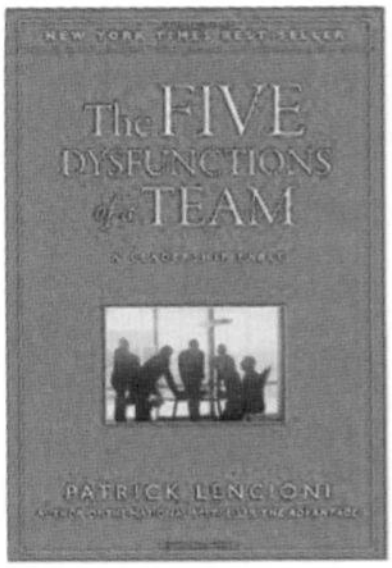

In his book "The Advantage" (Jossey-Bass, 2012), Lencioni released the results of 12,000 team assessments. The following table shows the percentage of times that teams scored low. The scoring system produced three categories — low, medium and high. The results showed in 65 percent of teams, accountability was missing. It also showed 40 percent of teams lacked trust.

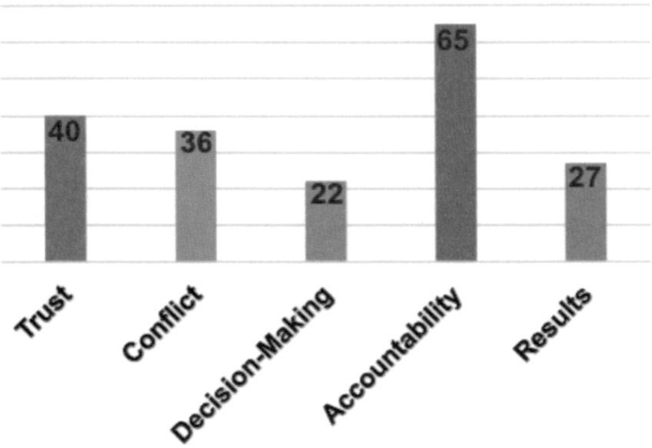

CHECKPOINT 17

Every year we spend money on targeted leadership programs to develop bench strength and capability.

Lencioni's book was based on a fable, and we are not sure about the validity of the construct. At PBC, we designed our own high-performing team assessment, which can be completed online by team members. We see teams as having two critical components: performance and culture.

Performance consists of:	Culture consists of:
➢ Strategy ➢ Innovation ➢ Accountability ➢ Leading change ➢ Collaboration ➢ Results	➢ Resilience ➢ Emotional intelligence ➢ Meeting effectiveness ➢ Professional conflict ➢ Trust ➢ Communication

Our research uniquely shows how teams can be improved by developing an action plan from the menu below. These options come from analysing the written feedback from teams that have used our assessment. The options, ranked in order of prevalence (highest to lowest), are:

IMPROVE COMMUNICATIONS	Open and honest communications, keep us updated, share the big picture, share information, communicate decisions
CLEARER VISION, STRATEGY AND GOALS	Clear KPIs, a clear business plan, shared sense of purpose, clear direction, disciplined strategic reviews
MORE COLLABORATION	One team approach, no silos, less "them and us," all on the same page, working together with one goal
TEAM BUILDING	Understand each other, share our strengths and weaknesses, build self-awareness, team-building exercises, understand each other's personalities and work styles
MORE ACCOUNTABILITY	Challenge each other constructively, correct poor behaviour, stronger KPI reviews, hold people responsible, challenge poor performers
MORE SOCIAL OCCASIONS	Social events, more time together as friends, social activity, regular social occasions
PROCESS IMPROVEMENT	Streamline processes, standardise processes, continuous improvement, improve internal processes, consistency
CELEBRATE SUCCESSES	Celebrate achievements, more recognition and reward, recognise good performance, celebrate wins and milestones
BETTER MEETINGS	Straightforward agendas, improved punctuality, better attendance, no wasting time, regular meetings for catch-ups
REGULAR MEETING RHYTHM	Regular business reviews, regular team meetings, stronger planning process, separate operational and strategic reviews, strategic discussions
MORE RESOURCES	Need more resources, align resources to business objectives, better resource planning, better sharing of resources
SET PRIORITIES	Be clear on priorities from the beginning, allocate time according to priorities, better manage competing priorities, honest discussions on priorities
REGULAR FEEDBACK	Continuous performance feedback, constructive feedback, ongoing feedback on how to do better
TACKLE THE DIFFICULT ISSUES	More healthy debate, challenge each other, discuss the hard issues, don't avoid conflict
CLEARER ROLES AND RESPONSIBILITIES	Clarify exactly who does what, clearly define job descriptions, get people to take ownership, understanding each other's roles and responsibilities

We get teams to self-assess, prioritise the opportunities, and implement an action plan. We also get team members to review the performance and behaviour of the team by giving feedback around keep doing, stop doing and start doing.

This chapter focused on the importance of building effective leadership. As we said, leadership drives engagement, and engagement drives performance. As a business grows, it is critical to grow the talent pool. Investment in leadership is often an investment in the bottom line. Engagement enhances sales, revenue, safety, productivity and profitability. It reduces absenteeism and turnover.

Chapter 3 — Building Business Performance

In this chapter, we will focus on the six key result areas of building business performance.

1. Having a Strategic Planning Cycle
Having a robust and strategic **planning cycle** with quarterly reviews is the key to being strategic, not just operational. Managers have to work *on* the business, not just *in* the business. The one-page business plan describes what winning looks like, and helps provide clarity and focus. Financial and non-financial goals are needed to achieve a balanced scorecard. The focus needs to be both short term and long term.
2. Building a Performance Culture
A performance culture helps the business plan succeed. Culture can be guided by organisational values, and these should be supported by articulating desirable and undesirable employee behaviours. Values without behaviours can be useless. A performance culture drives discretionary effort, productivity and customer engagement, whereas a culture of legacy or entitlement can destroy a business.
3. Achieving Employee Engagement
Employee engagement is based on the effectiveness of recruitment, induction, development, motivation and retention. Hire hard and manage easy. Companies should aim to be an employer of choice or a great place to work, because engagement pays. It delivers on safety, productivity, sales, profitability and retention. Engagement is most impacted by managers (this should be measured), followed by team culture and job fit.

4. Achieving Customer Engagement
Customer engagement is crucial to building loyalty, cross-selling and receiving referrals. Customers want functional and emotional value, which drive repeat business. Functional value is defined by price, value, quality and reliability. Emotional value is created around the service experience, good communication, and relationships built on trust. Customer surveys should be used to measure engagement and identify improvement opportunities.
5. Delivering Service and Operational Excellence
Most businesses have traditionally had 30 percent waste and inefficiency through errors and double handling. Re-work is the enemy. Businesses need to adopt the philosophy of **"get it right, first time, every time."** Quality improvement tools should be used to work toward zero defects on key processes. This will drive productivity, efficiency and cycle time. Supply chain management and partnering important suppliers is critical.
6. Executing the Strategy
This involves having discipline around KPIs and a regular strategic meeting rhythm. **Accountability** must be strong. Poor performance should be called out. **Leading change** successfully and dealing with employees' emotions on this journey is critical for reinventing the business and coping with a turbulent, disruptive external environment. Execution is a form of competitive advantage when carried out better than the competition.

Having a Strategic Planning Cycle

Some organisations do strategic planning really well — others not so well. And they probably rely on budgets alone. The biggest success we have with clients resulted from introducing a rigorous annual planning cycle. It starts with planning 12 months ahead in which the anchor is a one- or two-day executive retreat to work on the business by painting a picture of what success looks like in the short and medium term.

> CHECKPOINT 18
>
> Our business plan provides a clear vision of what winning looks like.

At this retreat, business intelligence is shared so participants can review recent performance, do a competitor comparison, and study the impact of industry trends. This includes employee and customer surveys, a SWOT analysis (strengths and weaknesses internally, opportunities and threats externally) and information from futurists.

> CHECKPOINT 19
>
> We have a rolling (three- to five-year) strategic plan supported by a robust one-year plan.

Determining the participants for retreats is a golden opportunity. In past decades, it was only senior executives involved, but now we look for opportunities to broaden the group. Some organisations create space for middle managers, while others invite applications from employees. For some of our smaller clients (up to 40 employees) everyone gets involved and it becomes a very special day on the calendar, often with a social activity in the evening.

> CHECKPOINT 20
>
> We have a one-page executive summary business plan, which is used to provide clarity and accountability.

The outcome is typically a high-level three- to five-year view of what winning looks like based on a balanced scorecard (financial and non-financial targets), but more along the lines of the Baldrige model so leadership and culture is included. We then turn this into a one-year plan, so the objectives are very tangible and immediate.

The idea of the one-page plan is to provide clarity and accountability. In years gone by, organisations wasted time developing mission and vision statements, putting employees to sleep. They were very rarely measurable or motivational. We would rather have a succinct purpose statement, such as "We save lives," as exists for a fire and rescue organisation. The one-page plan becomes a storytelling tool for executives to engage middle management and the workforce. We look for rational engagement so people understand the bigger picture, the KPIs and their role and responsibilities. Accountability then becomes easier.

> CHECKPOINT 21
>
> All business units/ teams have second-tier plans that are aligned with the master business plan.

> CHECKPOINT 22
>
> We have a rigorous strategic planning cycle in place.

For the private sector, financials are paramount. This includes both top-line and bottom-line numbers. The top line is made up of revenue targets associated with organic and inorganic growth. The bottom line is about profit. The rest of the plan should cover critical success factors where the organisation is continuously improving. This can include leadership, people, customers, operations and culture.

One of our golden rules in facilitating these retreats is to spend 50 percent of the time on strategy and 50 percent on team building. Team building is not about playing golf or rock climbing, but about creating a high-performing team where the shared goals and culture within the group are strong. We often use the concept of "one team, one plan."

> CHECKPOINT 23
>
> Our revenue and profit performance projections look sound.

Out of the master plan come the second-tier plans, so we create a cascading effect from top to bottom. We translate the high-level objectives into KPIs for all of the business units. Budget also follows strategy, so that resources and priorities are crystal clear. The launch of the plan then becomes critical. Typically the CEO will do a roadshow where they tell the story. Many will hand out the one-page plan, or talk about the purpose statement. Some will talk about the aspirational revenue goals and how these will be achieved. The launch of the plan should create passion, energy and buy-in.

CHECKPOINT 24

We conduct quarterly reviews of the strategic plan.

Best practice is then to sponsor various leadership development activities to deliver the strategic plan. For example, if one of the goals is to be an employer of choice with high levels of engagement, the managers could be targeted around the development of their resilience and people skills (EQ). Their technical knowledge and cognitive ability are pretty much fixed, but there is plenty to do toward developing social and emotional behaviours that make others feel valued and engaged. Many leadership programs waste so much money by not being aligned with the organisational strategy. Indeed, many MBA programs do very little to build the EQ component of leadership, they simply focus on more subject matter expertise.

CHECKPOINT 25

At these reviews, we spend 50 percent of our time reviewing strategy, and 50 percent building a high-performing team.

Quarterly (off-site) reviews are a must. Sometimes, there is a benefit having the review off-site to avoid distractions from being in the office. This is to encourage the 90-day review where the leadership get up on the balcony to look at the dance floor. Once this cycle of planning takes hold — it takes about two years — it becomes second nature, and people ask, "How did we ever get by without it?" It becomes a discipline making leaders strategic, not just operational. The following diagram illustrates some of the key components of a strategic planning operating rhythm. The planning day is the key part of the year where performance against the previous year is reviewed, and the new one-year and three- to five-year plans are signed off. Surveys and business intelligence precede the planning event to inform the workshop.

Budgets and second-tier plans follow. The plans are launched to create engagement. Leadership programs are designed to build capability to deliver the plan. Quarterly reviews are locked into the calendar. Other key activities are scheduled into the 12-month planning cycle.

At the quarterly reviews, half of the time should be spent reviewing strategy, and the other half reviewing the team. The concept of reviewing the team is new to 90 percent of executives. The goal is to build trust through self- and other-awareness. The focus is on achieving a high-performing culture that enables results.

The focus on the team can include:

- Sharing one's life history (two highs and two lows).
- Sharing the results of personality assessments in the context of a team-building session.
- Sharing 360° results for individuals and the team.
- Conducting a high-performing team assessment.

CHECKPOINT 26

Our culture and strategy encourage innovation, and we are good at implementing new ideas.

- Running a session on emotional intelligence and how to learn new personal and social skills.
- Running a session on good judgement and how to improve our decision-making processes.
- Running a session on resilience (executive stamina) so that all the managers have positive thoughts and good energy levels by making time for recovery.
- Giving behavioural feedback to each other around what to keep doing, stop doing and start doing.
- Giving behavioural feedback about what the team needs to keep doing, stop doing and start doing.

The outcome from the planning retreats is obviously a focus on the big picture, which is typically a strategy for winning. The road map for success for the private sector is about sustainable revenue growth underpinned by sound margins. In the public sector it is about how they make a difference, and being best in class when benchmarked against similar organisations.

When looking at revenue growth, organisations need to consider customer retention, cross-selling, greater market share, new products and new markets. For non-organic growth, acquisitions can also be part of the strategic planning.

Some organisations take a strategic view of how they compete in the marketplace. This can centre on either operational excellence, innovation or customer intimacy. The operational excellence model competes on cost, where the goal is to give the customer the cheapest price (McDonald's). The innovation model competes on being first to market with new products and services (Apple). The customer intimacy model is based on the strength of the brand and the associated customer loyalty in selling more (typically expensive) offerings (Louis Vuitton). The challenge is to build a point of difference in the value offering to the customer.

CHECKPOINT 27

Our results show that we are an employer of choice.

Consider the strategic planning model used by the Ritz-Carlton hotel chain. The Ritz-Carlton won the Baldrige Award twice. Their strategic approach embraces five elements:

- Grow from 70 hotels to 100
- Employee engagement
- Customer engagement
- Operational/service excellence
- Profitability

This model is simple, elegant and comprehensive. Ninety percent of our clients say that they can work with this model.

Jack Welch popularised a business planning model in his time as CEO at General Electric. He talked about three key strategic components:

- Winning starts with a strategic picture that inspires you.
- Get the right people in the right jobs to drive the picture forward.
- Grab best practices from anywhere, and learn/adapt and improve them.

Building a Performance Culture

Culture can deliver or defeat strategy. It can be friend or foe. Organisations should aim to be an employer of choice or a great place to work. This can be measured through an engagement survey, staff turnover, 360° reviews of managers and by high-performing team assessments. We want managers and people to be a source of competitive advantage. They deliver on strategy, operational excellence and customer centricity. All three are key elements in sustainable financial success.

You can quickly get a feel for an organisation's culture by examining whether it is a performance culture or an entitlement culture. Many airlines with long histories are what we call "legacy businesses." That is, their pay, conditions and work practices were set decades ago, and now they struggle to compete against new startup airlines. This involves massive challenges for a business with a brownfields culture (i.e., decades old) trying to compete against a greenfields culture (i.e., new entrants with contemporary practices).

CHECKPOINT 28

Our values are supported by behaviours; our employees know the behaviours we want and don't want.

In the past, organisations would attempt to build a high-performing culture based on values. These values come from a five-star management retreat, and often plucked out of the air. They would be generic values such as integrity, professionalism, community, customer service and innovation. Values without behaviours are pretty much useless.

The Ritz-Carlton is a good case study of a business that understands the importance of living the values and behaviours. Their credo is "We are Ladies and Gentlemen serving Ladies and Gentlemen." They translated their credo into 12 fundamental workplace behaviours that are reviewed for 10 minutes at the start of every shift (e.g., "I build strong relationships and create Ritz-Carlton guests for life"). This is to ensure employees are frequently reminded of tangible behaviours that will allow them to achieve the Ritz-Carlton values. The Ritz-Carlton also takes culture very seriously, and has the most rigorous approach to using values and behaviours to create strong levels of employee and customer engagement. As a result, employee turnover is around 20 percent, whereas the industry average is 60 percent.

CHECKPOINT 29

We employ robust recruitment systems to hire the right people.

Other organisations not only state the behaviours they want, but also the behaviours they will not tolerate. One of our clients, a fire and rescue organisation, said they do not value:

- Backstabbing
- People not pulling their weight
- Complainers who continually run the job down
- Abuse of sick leave
- People putting their second job first
- Theft

These unacceptable behaviours are often the "sacred cows." In "Sacred Cows Make the Best Burgers" (Warner Books, 1996), Kriegel and Brandt argue that sacred cows are the old policies, practices, procedures and paperwork that stifle productivity and profits.

Behaviours are best identified in an employee engagement survey where people write down the best and worst behaviours seen at work. We have been using this employee engagement survey methodology for more than a decade. It highlights the best and worst of an organisation's culture. The sacred cows have evolved over many years, and often go unchallenged. The two most common sacred cows are lack of teamwork and lack of commitment. These sacred cows must be challenged if one is to build a high-performing culture.

The values and behaviours need to be owned by employees. They should be part of the selection and induction process and reviewed regularly. They can become a part of the performance management and review process (i.e., are employees living the values and delivering against the job description?).

Our research shows the two most important values for employees are teamwork and commitment. Teamwork involves friendship, helping each other, caring for each other, working together across boundaries, and pursuing common goals. Lack of teamwork involves passing the buck, "them and us" attitudes, infighting, small-mindedness and silo mentality. Commitment involves having a good work ethic, going the extra mile, taking personal ownership of problems, and giving discretionary effort. Lack of commitment involves poor work ethics, laziness, slack attitudes and shirking responsibility.

If an organisation is customer facing, customer service can also be an important value. If the organisation works in a dangerous industry, safety must feature as one of the values. Apart from these four values, which come from hundreds of employee engagement surveys where staff write down the best and worst behaviours seen at work, any other values are made up by management. We should challenge them for their relevancy. If an organisation is genuinely seeking to drive innovation as key to future success, then we could understand why this would be a value to help build such a culture. But if it is a motherhood statement, its relevance can be questioned. The values need to be real for employees.

CHECKPOINT 30

We formally induct new hires and use a probationary period to assess both likeability and capability.

Employee value propositions (EVPs) are proving quite popular. When defining an EVP, it's important to conduct employee or prospective employee research to establish what would attract and retain people. This

EVP then becomes part of the organisation's brand and culture. It establishes a value proposition for new and existing employees, and is aimed at recruiting the right people, reducing staff turnover, and building engagement. The EVP is critical for organisations with significant staff turnover, because the cost of absenteeism and resignations are enormous. It is also a must-do for organisations that want to be a truly great place to work.

Starbucks did an employee engagement survey some years ago asking, "what are the top three things that brought you here?" and "what are the top three things that keep you here?" Another organisation surveyed their 20,000 people to establish the most important things for retention and motivation. They built a story around the four key result areas:

- Show me the work
- Show me the flexibility
- Show me the money
- Show me the security

CHECKPOINT 31

We achieve top-quartile results in our employee engagement surveys.

This helped build the brand and tell the story to attract, engage and retain people. If the values and behaviours are genuine, they can be used in performance reviews to assess whether people are walking the talk and being role models. Remember, you can easily assess people by looking at their behaviour and performance.

Achieving Employee Engagement

Getting the right managers to lead a team is critical for employee engagement. Employees who quit an organisation typically quit the manager, the team culture, or the job fit. The challenge is to find, motivate and retain the best people. It starts by having a culture and process around "hire hard, manage easy." Organisations should have a clear picture of who the right staff are when recruiting. This can involve the use of assessment centres and personality profiling. The probationary period should be used rigorously before permanency is granted. If employees are working in a team or client facing, they need to be both likeable and capable. Likeable means being resilient and having people skills so others will see them as being warm, approachable, positive and engaged. Being capable involves job mastery so others trust your competency. It requires a good work ethic and technical competence. These two aspects should be screened for during selection.

CHECKPOINT 32

The bottom 10 percent of employees are identified regularly and either improve, or are removed in a timely manner.

Managers should also recruit and develop around the concept of warmth and competence. Their cognitive skills, technical abilities and work ethic are already well defined, and the challenge is building high-performing teams with engaged employees. Managers soon discover that 80 percent of their problems are people issues. Their journey is toward becoming a part-time psychologist. They need to be able to read other people like a book. In their journey to becoming a manager, technical competence, work ethic, self-awareness and self-regulation are key. Once they become a manager, interpersonal skills are important in understanding, influencing and motivating others. These are relationship-management skills rather than self-management skills.

CHECKPOINT 33

Our one-page plan is used as a communication tool for all employees.

Engaged people are both rationally and emotionally engaged. The rational component is that they understand and support the business plan/KPIs and are motivated around operational excellence and customer service. They understand their job description and responsibilities. They bring discretionary effort to the table.

The emotional engagement component is they respect their manager, love their team, and bring a positive attitude and good energy levels to work every day. Their net promoter score when recommending the organisation to friends as a great place to work is high.

CHECKPOINT 34

We give our customers a high degree of functional value around price, quality and reliability.

Communication is always a challenge to keep engagement levels high. Employees typically want to know what is going on (put the cards on the table), need this in face-to-face meetings (not emails), and want to be consulted and involved (get staff input). We have never heard of a workforce complaining about over-communication. Key competencies for managers must include communication skills. The business plan should form the basis of a communication strategy containing high-level goal updates and lower-level KPI reviews. We teach our clients to communicate the business plan "seven times, in seven ways" to get the message through.

CHECKPOINT 35

We give our customers a high level of emotional value around service, communications and trust.

Another big issue that comes up in employee engagement surveys and 360° reviews is the need to hold people accountable and in particular, challenge poor performers. One bad apple in a team can create major issues. The problem is compounded when there are multiple poor performers sharing their misery with others. For many years, we focused on the need to address poor performers. It can be part of the business plan (e.g., "good performance will be recognised, poor performance will be challenged" — no passengers). These passengers should be identified at quarterly reviews with a goal of improving or removing them in the next 90-day cycle. We use a

CHECKPOINT 36

We are a provider of choice for the majority of our customers.

six-step process to train managers on how to have the difficult conversation:

- Issue — the performance or behaviour to be addressed
- Expectations — how these are not being met
- Impact — the negative effect on performance or team
- Explanation — get the other person's point of view
- Consequences — the next steps if this is not fixed
- Agreement — the details of the way forward

This six-step model allows for the difficult conversation to take place in a professional manner without emotions. It encourages two-way dialogue and finishes with an outcome. Many management teams embrace this six-step model with enthusiasm.

Jim Collins in "Good to Great" (HarperCollins, 2001) said the following:

"Letting the wrong people hang around is unfair to all the right people, who often find themselves compensating for the wrong people's inadequacies. Get the wrong people off the bus."

We often challenge our clients to identify their bottom 10 percent and to think about how these people could be improved or removed as part of the quarterly strategic reviews.

Achieving Customer Engagement

Creating engaged customers creates profitable businesses. Engaged customers are happy with the service experience and functional utility of the products purchased. They also have an emotional connection to the organisation, which is often called brand loyalty. Customer needs are twofold. They want functional value and they want emotional value. Functional value relates to the price paid and the value received for the service or good with a focus on two key result areas: quality and timeliness.

CHECKPOINT 37

Support services add significant value to our business.

Emotional value is gained through trust and peace of mind where there is a relationship involved beyond the transactional piece of business. Emotional value generates positive net promoter scores, repeat business, cross-selling opportunities and referrals.

In the old days, Henry Ford used to say, "You can have any colour car you want, provided it is black." The focus was on product, not customer. These days, customers have a choice and are prepared to shop around.

Some customers just want cheap. This will drive a culture of operational excellence in business around driving costs down. Other customers want new products, and this will drive a culture of innovation and being first to market. Finally, some customers want a prestigious brand, and are prepared to pay a premium. This drives organisations to focus on reputation, image and loyalty.

The Baldrige model talks about customer engagement. Different organisations express this in their business plans as customer relationship management, customer centricity, customer intimacy, customer stickiness or brand loyalty. It is all aimed at winning the hearts and minds of the customers. To achieve emotional engagement, the provider of choice needs to be emotionally intelligent. Cognitive capacity and technical know-how are not enough. They simply get you in the door.

CHECKPOINT 38

The results of our customer surveys are very good.

Everyone has a customer. Customers are either external or internal. In the private sector, external customers are the ones who pay. In the public sector, external customers are people who benefit or potentially benefit from a service. Internal customers are typically relevant for support services (human resources, information technology and finance). Internal providers must be held accountable by their internal customers. Too often, they do their own thing or do not add enough value. Some organisations use service-level agreements to drive internal service standards and accountabilities.

CHECKPOINT 39

Lifelong customer loyalty is our goal, and our high retention rate reflects that effort.

The voice of the customer should be used to establish customer priorities, preferences and satisfaction with current performance. This can be done through customer surveys (some of the big banks use the net promoter score). Customer surveys are very powerful. Telephone interviews work best to generate a good response rate and an open discussion. Key questions can include:

- What are the best things about this organisation?
- What are the worst things about this organisation?
- How do you rate this organisation on price?
- How do you rate this organisation on quality?
- How do you rate this organisation against their competitors?
- What are your future business intentions?
- How much trust and loyalty are there?

The results of these surveys can inform the business planning cycle and be used as staff feedback to drive improvement. There can also be a KPI around the overall satisfaction level.

One of the great things we have done with some clients is to bring the voice of the customer inside the business. We do this by bringing a real customer to present at the business planning retreat or to a leadership group. The audience is normally spellbound listening to every word from the customer. The key message can have a powerful impact and help set the agenda.

Service standards can also be a powerful way of becoming customer centric. Many years ago, we worked with Qantas baggage handlers at the Sydney Airport to produce KPIs for service levels. We included the following:

- We will deliver priority baggage in five to nine minutes.
- We will deliver economy baggage within nine to 15 minutes.
- We will aim for 95 percent on-time departure.
- We will aim for a mishandled baggage statistic of four bags or less per 1,000 handled.

> CHECKPOINT 40
>
> We achieve our service and operational excellence goals.

Many service organisations will recruit employees with a service orientation. This can be helped through personality profiling as part of the assessment process. Some years ago, we did a major Hogan study of what makes for great customer service staff and found the following:

1. They have strong people skills and warmth comes naturally ... they will get along easily with customers.
2. They love working in teams, networking and belonging ... they will be drawn to customers.
3. They have strong composure and stress management ... they can handle difficult customers.
4. They are hedonistic and want the good things in life ... they will create great customer experiences.
5. They are not driven by ambition, power or money ... they are happiest with people.

Service organisations must recruit, develop and motivate staff to deliver the desired customer experience. We want engaged employees serving engaged, loyal customers.

Delivering Service and Operational Excellence

When the first excellence frameworks were created in 1988, called Quality Awards, such was the focus on improving quality as the key to global competitiveness. Total Quality Management was the name most commonly associated with quality initiatives. The aim was to eliminate rework and "get it right, first time, every time." Quality assurance programs, often associated with the International Standards Organisation, would drive certification as a certificate of competency around quality and systems.

CHECKPOINT 41

We have performance standards in place for key processes so that we avoid deviations.

W. Edwards Deming is often regarded as the father of quality, and he was passionate about tackling waste through process improvement. Deming was born in 1900 and became famous in Japan in the early 1950s for helping industry to rebuild on quality principles at a time when mass production based on quantity was the prevailing wisdom in the western world. The Japanese were so impressed that they created a national quality award and named it after Deming. By 1980, quality Japanese products were beating locally made products in the USA. It did not take Ford (and other famous names) long to get in on the act. Ford engaged Deming at the age of 80 to kick-start their quality journey.

Deming argued that all organisations generate considerable waste — his estimate was between 30-40 percent. This waste is made up of rework, defects, errors, delays, double-handling, late deliveries and lack of reliability. Business obviously sees a strong case for reducing waste and aiming for zero defects. This enhances customer satisfaction, encourages employee empowerment, and delivers bottom-line financial results.

CHECKPOINT 42

We use quality improvement tools to work toward zero defects on key processes.

CHECKPOINT 43

We work strategically with suppliers for mutual gain.

When we consult Qantas, they focus the workforce on safety and punctuality as their model of operational excellence. Federal Express have a credo, "The world, on time," to drive process improvement and superior performance.

In the early 1990s, the words "best practice" and "continuous improvement" (Kaizen) became popular. For the first time, concepts such as KPIs and benchmarking emerged. Business process re-engineering was also popular. In more recent times, the language of Lean Six Sigma and supply chain management is more common.

Six Sigma is a set of techniques and tools for process improvement. It was developed by Motorola in 1986 and popularised by Jack Welch at General Electric. Six Sigma is a measure of defect-free products. The aim of Six Sigma is for 99.9996 percent of all process, products and services to be defect free.

CHECKPOINT 44

Our technology is up to date and efficient.

Businesses need to identify their critical processes aimed at delivering customer satisfaction and value. These critical processes need to be standardised to avoid duplication and waste. The challenge is to aim for 100 percent perfection. Easier said than done! Our employee engagement survey research shows that the five most common forms of waste are:

1. Human effort/rework (doing jobs twice, double handling, human error)

2. Time wasting/time delays (not managing time effectively, slow follow-up, chasing information)

3. Too much paperwork (duplication, unnecessary reports, paper trails)

4. Poor resources (old technology/equipment, too much down time)

5. Unproductive people (laziness, apathy, misuse of work time)

Our employee engagement survey research also shows that the five best ways to improve productivity are:

1. Everyone pulling their weight (employ the right people to start with, remove deadwood)

2. Improve morale/make people feel valued (create a culture of trust and support, have positive attitudes)

3. Incentive pay/bonus (productivity pay, gain sharing, rewards for good performers)

4. More teamwork/less "them and us" (common goals, departments working together)

5. Continuous improvement/less rework (improve processes/ systems, reduce waste)

You will notice that a lot of the process improvement opportunities are related to culture, engagement and accountability.

Suppliers and contractors often contribute significantly to the production of goods and services. Outsourcing has been a strong contributor to improved performance. The approach to suppliers should be a partnering one. Efficiencies and savings are critical to the relationship, but it should be based on mutual benefits.

Innovation is also a key aspect of driving business excellence. It simply means implementing new ideas or taking new products to the market. Technology has been the backbone of innovation. The life cycle of products has been greatly reduced, due to the rapid pace of advancements in technology. Innovation can be used to improve existing processes for core services and products. It can also be used to design new services and products, and for entering new markets. At the turn of the century, Apple, Google, 3M and Toyota were highly regarded as global innovators.

Employees and teams need to take ownership and accountability for their processes. Standardisation and accuracy are key. Lean process management strategies can help reduce costs and cycle time. Six Sigma (99.9996 percent quality) can assist defect reduction and improve product yield. Supply chain management involves working strategically with suppliers and partners for mutual gain. The journey towards best practice service and operational excellence is a race without a finish line.

Executing the Strategy

Many books have been written about execution. Actually implementing a strategic plan can be a source of competitive advantage if it is done well. This refers to the fact that many organisations have a business plan collecting dust on a shelf. The default position is still to be operational, not strategic. It is important to have an annual planning cycle in place so that strategy and execution become a way of life, not a random event. This can be achieved by the following:

- Creating an **exciting three to five year strategy** which defines goals around success, growth, stakeholder engagement and service/operational excellence.
- Translating the broader strategy into **one-year plans** with clearly defined goals, milestones, measures and accountabilities ... who, what, when, where?
- Cascading the master plan into **second- and third-tier plans** to take the helicopter view down to business unit levels, so there is a clear line of sight from top to bottom.
- Holding managers accountable for their goals/KPIs in a formal and regular manner. Managers are evaluated for both their performance and behaviour.

CHECKPOINT 45

All teams have KPIs in place, covering areas such as financials, operations, customers and employees.

- Communicating to employees a one-page summary business plan to create engagement and accountability. The launch of the plan should be energising.
- Communicating the strategy **“seven times, in seven ways”** to get a high level of awareness and ownership.
- Holding disciplined management team meetings to focus their time separately between strategic and operational agendas.
- Reviewing progress regularly — at least quarterly. At the quarterly reviews, spend 50 percent of the time reviewing strategy, and the other 50 percent on team culture.
- Sponsoring a leadership program to build capability to deliver the goals. Emerging leaders are targeted to build self-awareness and new competencies.

Execution is a form of competitive advantage. It requires discipline around implementation. The advantage comes from the fact that most of your competitors will not be executing well. The key focus should be on measurement, accountability, regular reviews and effectiveness in leading change.

If you do not measure performance, you can not improve it. What you measure should provide a laser focus. Classic measurement systems are centred on KPIs. These indicators can tell us current levels of performance so we can track improvement and the achievement of goals from the business plan. KPIs can tell us whether or not we are on track against the high-level objectives. Some organisations use a dashboard of KPIs coloured green, amber or red to track progress.

CHECKPOINT 46

All managers are measured annually through 360° reviews, employee engagement surveys or high-performing team assessments.

A strong culture of measurement should be embedded in organisations so there is literacy around numeracy. If we revisit the Baldrige model, KPIs are needed in five areas:

CHECKPOINT 47

Our structure supports the strategy, we don't have any silos.

1. Product and process results
2. Customer-focused results
3. Workforce-focused results
4. Leadership and governance results
5. Financial and market results

In the last decade, many organisations have made inroads into creating strong measurement systems. We think an area of focus for the next five years will be measuring leadership effectiveness and using such metrics to determine the fate of these leaders. Leadership effectiveness can be measured in several ways:

- Engagement surveys can pinpoint the well-being of a business unit/department, which is a reflection of the manager.
- A high-performing team assessment can tell you how well a leader is managing the team.
- A 360° assessment will capture the performance and behaviour of a manager, as seen by colleagues at work. Personality assessments will help explain this behaviour and performance.

The big challenge is to make these measurement outcomes a critical platform for reviewing and rewarding management performance. It is still the case today most managers are reviewed largely on service/operational and financial metrics, and the broader engagement metrics play second fiddle. The lead indicator should be the behaviour of the manager in building and maintaining a team. The lag indicator should be the output from the team. A 50/50 split is worthy of consideration. This means managers can be reviewed and rewarded 50 percent for behaviour and 50 percent for results. The behaviour is living the values and being a role model.

KPIs are also pivotal to benchmarking. You can not compare your performance against previous years or against best in class if you do not have strong, accurate measures in place. There is much to be gained from benchmarking within the industry and against other industries. The concept is to establish best practice, learn from it, and sometimes to steal shamelessly from others.

CHECKPOINT 48

Our execution of the plan is supported by strong implementation processes.

KPIs are also a powerful way of cascading the business plan throughout the organisation. Once you have the business plans established at the level of first team (the executive group for the whole of the business) and second teams, anything further down can simply be a one-page plan consisting of four to six KPIs.

In their book "The Strategy-Focused Organization" (Harvard Business Press, 2001), Kaplan and Norton progressed their balanced scorecard framework into a tool to help implement strategy. They elaborated five key principles which help with execution:

1. Translate strategy into operational terms — you can not implement strategy unless you can describe it.
2. Align the organisation to the strategy — break down the silos.
3. Make strategy everyone's everyday job — communication/education, personal scorecards, team-based incentives.
4. Make strategy a continual process — introduce management meetings and reviews.
5. Mobilise change through strong, effective leadership — the single most important condition for success is the ownership and active involvement of the executive team.

The key to rigorous implementation is to be disciplined strategically. Once the planning cycle has been used for a couple of years, it should become second nature. It becomes a very

CHECKPOINT 49

Accountability standards are high throughout the business.

powerful habit. Accountability is key. Organisations need to do what they say in the strategic plan. A strong culture of accountability is needed. Remember, Patrick Lencioni's research around teams showed that 65 percent score low on accountability (Jossey-Bass, 2012). It is one of the biggest challenges we face. It is not just about a leader holding the team accountable. It is also about peer reviews, annual 360˚ assessments and team members giving each other feedback around keep doing, stop doing and start doing. Managers need to be held accountable for both behaviour and performance.

Building leadership and business capability can often involve a lot of change. Strategy regularly involves repositioning the business, changing the status quo, and taking people out of their comfort zones. Management has a huge responsibility to communicate and win the hearts and minds of employees. This can be very challenging given that one in three people are already disengaged.

If turbulence and disruption are framing the new business environment, then leading change becomes a leadership critical success factor. Most change programs under-deliver. When driving change, managers need to master the emotional and rational issues. The emotional side is allowing people to identify their feelings, and the rational side is the logical and compelling case for change.

John Kotter, who wrote "The Heart of Change" (Harvard Business School Press, 2002), is the world's leading guru on change. He has a very powerful quote:

"Our main finding is that the central issue is never strategy, structure, culture or systems. All those elements, and others, are important. But the core of the matter is always about changing the behaviour of people, and behaviour change happens in highly successful situations mostly by speaking to people's feelings."

When working with management teams, we often get them to share their feelings and emotions in the context of the current business environment. We often get a mixture of both positive and negative. It's a good way of sharing and testing for resilience and engagement. Positive characteristics often include: highly motivated, hardworking, excited, enthusiastic and loyal. Negative characteristics can include: tired, exhausted, frustrated, burned out and defeated. This process is a good way of acknowledging people's feelings and taking the pulse.

Kotter estimates that around 70 percent of change initiatives fail. This number comes from Kotter's research in 1995. It was confirmed by seperate research from McKinsey & Company in 2008. Great businesses understand leading change involves reacting to threats or opportunities as a "burning platform." Kotter uses the concept of the burning platform as creating urgency and momentum to change. This is often driven by the external environment, and can be political, economic, societal, technological, environmental or legislative. Great businesses can then tell a story to their employees about the need to move quickly, and they do this by having high levels of engagement and dealing with feelings and emotions.

The eight steps are as follows:

1. ***Increase urgency****. Craft and use a significant opportunity as a means for exciting people to sign up to change their organisation.*

2. ***Build the guiding team****. Assemble a group with the power and energy to lead and support a collaborative change effort.*

CHECKPOINT 50

We understand that change is permanent, and we deal with people's feelings/ emotions as part of the journey.

3. ***Get the vision right***. *Shape a vision to help steer the change effort and develop strategic initiatives to achieve that vision.*

4. ***Communicate for buy-in***. *Raise a large force of people who are ready, willing and have the urgency to drive change.*

5. ***Empower action***. *Remove obstacles to change, change systems or structures that pose threats to the achievement of the vision.*

6. ***Create short-term wins***. *Consistently produce, track, evaluate and celebrate volumes of small and large accomplishments — and correlate them to results.*

7. ***Do not let up***. *Hire, promote and develop employees who can implement the vision; reinvigorate the process with new projects, themes and volunteers.*

8. ***Make change stick***. *Articulate the connections between the new behaviours and organisational success, and develop the means to ensure leadership development and succession.*

Turbulence and disruption are now the new norms for the business world. Winning organisations will be those that can reinvent themselves faster than their competitors. Leading change is a key capability.

Our research shows leadership is responsible for creating engagement, and engagement pays. Leadership and engagement are measurable and can be improved. If you add business excellence disciplines, you should be well placed to outperform the competition. The CEO Checklist should help many managers to assess their business/business unit and develop an action plan for improvement.

Good luck!

Bibliography

Aon Hewitt 2015, *2015 Trends in Global Employee Engagement*. Available from file: http://www.aon.com/attachments/human-capital-consulting/2015-Trends-in-Global-Employee-Engagement-Report.pdf [19 November, 2015].

Chamorro-Premuzic, T 2013, *Confidence: Overcoming Low Self-Esteem, Insecurity, and Self-Doubt*, Penguin Group, New York.

Collins, J 2001, *Good to Great*, Random House Business Books, London, UK.

Covey, SR 2004, *The 7 Habits of Highly Effective People*, Pocket Books, London.

Covey, SR 2006, *The Speed of Trust*, Simon and Schuster, New York.

Duhigg, C 2012, *The Power of Habit*, Random House, New York.

Goleman, D 1995, *Emotional Intelligence: Why It Can Matter More Than IQ*, Bantam Books, New York.

Goldsmith, M & Reiter, M 2007, *What Got You Here, Won't Get You There: How Successful People Become Even More Successful*, Hyperion, London.

Heskett, JL; Jones, TO; Loveman, GW; Sasser, WE; & Schlesinger, LA 2008, *Putting the Service-Profit Chain to Work*, Harvard Business Review.

Kaplan, RS & Norton, DP 1996, *The Balanced Scorecard*, Harvard Business Review Press, Boston.

Kaplan, RS & Norton, DP 2001, *The Strategy-Focused Organization*, Harvard Business Press.

Kotter, J 2002, *The Heart of Change*, Harvard Business School Press.

Kriegel, RJ & Brandt, D 1996, *Sacred Cows Make the Best Burgers*, HarperCollinsPublishers, Sydney, Australia.

Lencioni, P 2002, *The Five Dysfunctions of a Team*, Jossey-Bass, U.S.

Lencioni, P 2012, *The Advantage*, Jossey-Bass, San Francisco.

Malone, C & Fiske, ST 2013, *The Human Brand: How We Relate to People, Products, and Companies,* Jossey-Bass, San Francisco.

Nutt, P 2002, *Why Decisions Fail*, Berret- Koehler Publishers,

Seldman, M & Seldman, J 2008, *Executive Stamina: How to Optimize Time, Energy, and Productivity to Achieve Peak Performance*, John Wiley & Sons, New Jersey.

Sorenson, S 2013, *How employee engagement drives growth*, Gallup Business Journal. Available from http://www.gallup.com/businessjournal/163130/employee-engagement-drives-growth.aspx [19 November, 2015].

Tichy, NM & Bennis, WG 2009, *Judgment: How Winning Leaders Make Great Calls*, Portfolio.

Welch, J 2005, Winning, HarperCollinsPublishers, London.